C0-ARS-622

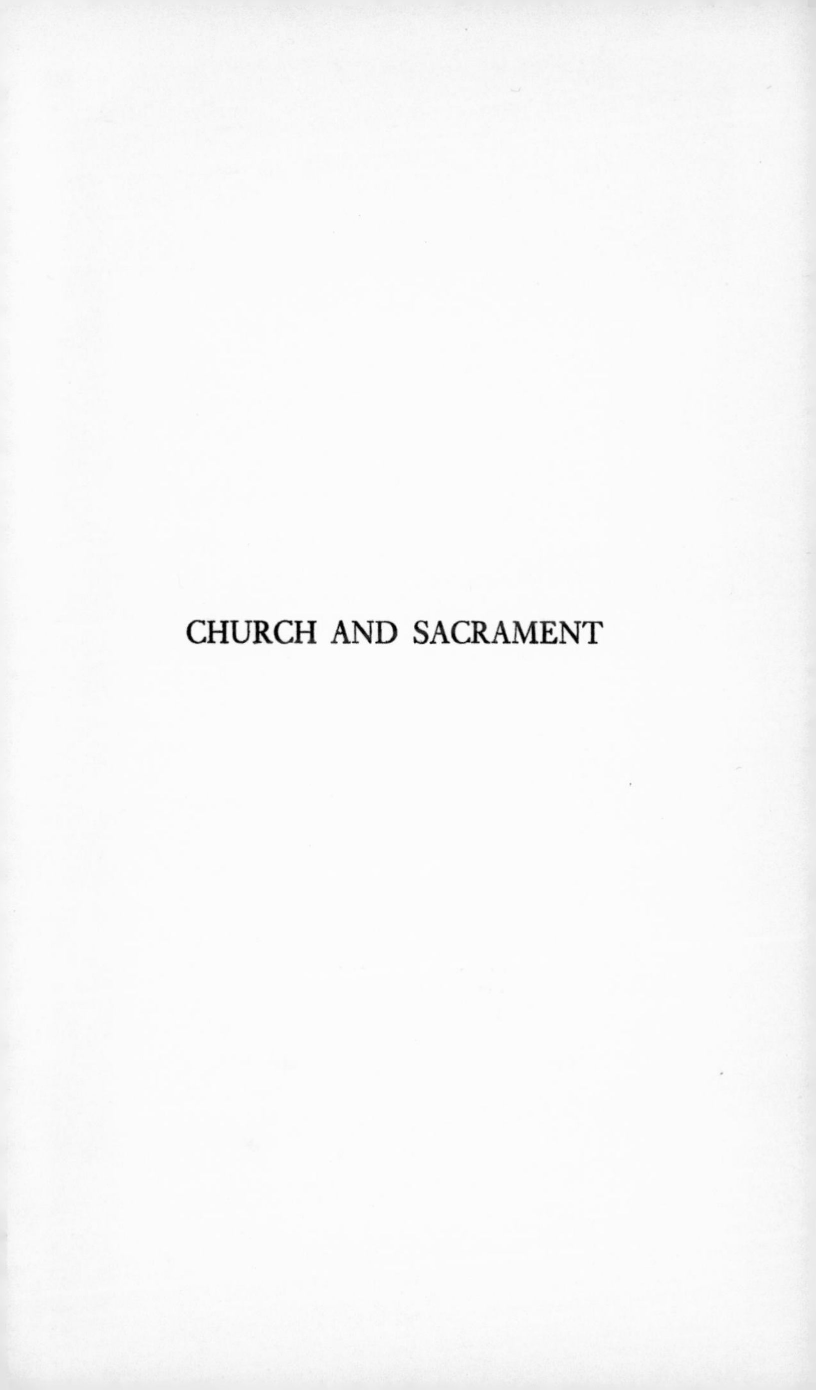

CHURCH AND SACRAMENT

CHURCH AND SACRAMENT

by Otto Semmelroth, S.J.

Translated by Emily Schossberger

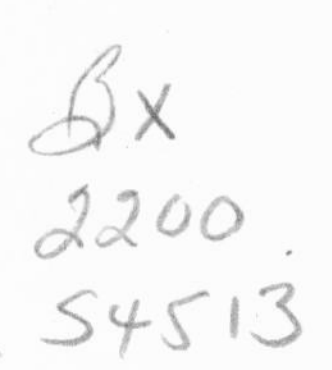

FIDES PUBLISHERS, INC.
NOTRE DAME, INDIANA

Nihil Obstat
Louis J. Putz, C.S.C.
University of Notre Dame

Imprimatur
Leo A. Pursley, D.D.
Bishop of Fort Wayne-South Bend

Church and Sacrament
is a translation of *Vom Sinn der Sakramente*,
published originally in German by Verlag Josef Knecht,
Carolusdruckerei GmbH., Frankfurt a. M., 1960

Otto Semmelroth S.J.: *Vom Sinn der Sakramente*
2. unveranderte Auflage

Imprimi potest
Coloniae, die 21 ianuarii 1963

Nik. Junk S.J.
Praep.Prov.Germ. Inf.

Manufactured in the Republic of Ireland

CONTENTS

CHAPTER TWO

CHAPTER THREE

Foreword

A man who has achieved maturity in his human development, through his own efforts, study, social position, and other factors, jealously guards the rights of his person. This is especially evident in the religious sphere where the personal, interior, and most essential aspect of the individual is called upon in a special way. Almost necessarily one confronts the question of how such a personal self relates to the sacramental bonds of the life of faith within the Church. This is an important question for all who are concerned with the realization of the Christian faith. It can only be answered by a deeper understanding of those life functions of the Church in which sacramental objectivity and personal commitment are demanded in equal measure. One must know how the proclamation of the word of God and the sacramental worship are intended by the God-man founder as the many-in-one form of the Church's life. The sacramental life functions themselves are rightly understood only from the perspective of the sacramental mystery of the Church whose actualization they are. One must recognize the meaning of the Church as a sign of salvation instituted by Christ.

This constitutes the link which binds together the four chapters of this book. They were developed from lectures given under the sponsorship of the Catholic Academic Association at the University of Bonn during the so-called 'Catholic Academic Week' in October of 1959, with the title 'The Church and the Sacraments.' Such a vast theme must naturally be condensed. Therefore, much of it can be presented only in essential outline. But such condensation in itself was a special challenge; since this was not simply an abridged listing of facts which could be presented in greater detail, but a true synthesis which by its own nature is worth discussing. This also means that what is stated here is not necessarily new in all its details. Theology has treated of it already, and the author has talked about it elsewhere. One or another of the chapters may bring out some new detail, at least in the sense in which details always shed new light if they are put into a new perspective. The aim of this short work, then, is to bring home to us the actual situation of the human person in relation to the sacramental life of the Church, which is the life of salvation.

Chapter One

The Church as Sign

The Church is both the subject and the object of our faith. It is a community of those who, as true believers, accept God's revelation, but it is also part of the content of that revelation. The Church is so much the *subject* of the believing encounter with God that it has been able to continue this life of faith for centuries without really reflecting on itself or acquiring self-understanding through theological research. Until recently theology, which has divided its subjects into different treatises, has had none for the Church.

That the Church could carry out its life according to its nature without concerning itself too much with an understanding of its being, certainly shows clearly that it lives and works on a different life principle than human thoughts and wills alone. Rather it lives on the strength of the Pentecostal Spirit which the risen Christ has breathed into it as a life principle. In fact, whenever the Church has at any time reflected upon the truth God revealed to it, it was at the same time reflecting upon itself. But with the development of its life through the centuries, and particularly under the impact of the heresies, the Church had to come to grips with the matter of understanding itself theologically. Its situation demands this: God in his revelation not only speaks to the Church, but also speaks to it about itself, revealing to it the divine mystery hidden in it. Thus the Church must accept itself from the all-revealing God, and of course also in the qualified way of faith which we call theology.

In accomplishing this task the Church through the course of history was forced into all kinds of misinterpretations of its nature and significance. As the human spirit attempts to understand and master reality, it is again and again led by misconceptions and errors to a closer approach to truth and a better penetration of its depths. Thus the many misconceptions of the Church have helped it to achieve a better grasp of its own nature. This is reason enough for us to speak in this first part of the chapter of partial understanding of the Church, but only in relation to the theme 'The Church as Sign.' The second part of the chapter will deal with the Church as a visible society within the framework of the three dimensions of ecclesial existence, which must always be kept in mind when the Church is to be explained according to its nature. This leads to the central theme, in the third part of this chapter: an explanation of the visible Church as sacramental sign.

MISCONCEPTIONS OF THE CHURCH

The Church may be misunderstood in two ways. In one way—which is our concern here—the existence of a validly established Church is accepted but its nature is misunderstood and is therefore presented incorrectly. Another way of misunderstanding, although not one within the framework of traditional Catholic belief, is exemplified by the Swiss-Reformed theologian, Emil Brunner, who wrote some years ago about 'the misconception of the Church.'[1] In his opinion it is a mistake to think that the *ecclesia* which, according to the New Testament, Christ grouped about himself was meant to be a social institution such as the Church is today. It is, he would say, therefore really due to a misunderstanding that there is a Church today at all.

On the contrary, Catholic belief firmly holds, that Christ, in the power of his words and works

[1] Emil Brunner, *Misunderstanding of the Church*, Philadelphia, 1953.

assembled a Church around himself, and that after his resurrection and ascension in the power of the Holy Spirit he sent that Church into history as a corporal institution to exert on this history a controlling and redeeming effect through the vitality of the divine life principle. There can be no misunderstanding about the fact that the Church exists. Since the Holy Spirit is not only the life principle but also the truth principle of the Church's knowledge of itself in faith, it cannot be essentially false or untrue. It is possible, however, that man by his own preference can fix his gaze so intensely on certain features in the face of the Church that this face would lose its vitality and harden into the mask of Medusa.

Such misconceptions of the Church are seen more exactly from two sides.

Individualistic Misconception

There is the view which takes the Church's measure solely from the free will of its individual members. This attitude is typical of the increasing individualism of modern times, especially concerning salvation, and in spite of the new 'awakening of the Church in our souls,'[2] it is characteristic of our times. We see here that many of the features instituted in the Church by Jesus Christ meet with a certain understanding on the part of modern man, and yet arouse at the same time new dangers of misunderstanding. The Church itself constantly stresses its social and institutional character, even calling itself a *societas perfecta*. This gives modern man, who recognizes the pluralistic character of human society, a certain understanding of the Church. Among the many different purposes for forming organizations why should not the religious purpose be the basis for formation of a church group? This then accounts for the appeal of the Church to the free moral decision of man: a pluralistic social order presupposes the free coming together of people for a commonly held end.

The understanding which modern humanism affords the Church as a religious institution often turns out to be no blessing, for it leads frequently to disastrous misconceptions. In spite of their different aims and diverse forms, pluralistic societies all have one thing in common: they are organizations whose existence depends on the decisions of many individuals. The resulting unity does not go beyond the moral community of many single wills united for a single purpose. Putting the Church in this category would be a misunderstanding of its nature. In the Church, community precedes the individual.

[2] Romano Guardini, *Vom Sinn der Kirche*, Mainz 1956.

The Church does not owe its existence to the decision of individual Christians, but individuals can determine themselves to be Christian—this word being understood in its full grace-laden sense—because and to the extent that they are in the living union of the Church. The essential common bond of the Church is not the religious will of the individuals who come together for a common goal, but the spirit of God whose grace binds individuals together in a kind of organic unity.

The understanding of the sacramental mystery of the Church and of the unity of the Mystical Body of Christ which blossomed anew after the First World War, has certainly opened up for many the way to a better understanding of the Church. But this new understanding has been weakened by modern personalism, which continues the individualistic emphasis with different nuances and through a misunderstanding of freedom exaggerates the interior and existential character of man's commitment to God.

It is easy to understand that there can be no question of a Church as a sign of salvation instituted by Christ, where the existence of the Church is dependent upon the decision of the individual (even one animated by the Holy Spirit).

Collectivistic Misconception

The Church may appear to be more easily understood as a sign of salvation instituted by Christ when viewed from the opposite direction: namely, from the perspective of an objectively existing society which automatically confers salvation on its members. Here too, in this near magical conception of the Church, its character as a sign is obscured. For what is proper to a sign is too little observed here: that is, it must be meaningful to the spirit of man so that it challenges the attitude of his will.

We should not explain away this magical notion of the Church by attributing it to childish or ignorant people. The intellectual, proud in the possession of his individuality, will certainly not like to admit that in order to be assured of peace with the powers of the next world he trusts in the efficacy of the Church, working as a thoroughly magical agent independent of personal decisions. Yet, is this temptation so rare? When free decisions are a risk, in the realm of everyday life where consequences cannot be calculated, most of us seek ' insurance ' of some kind for our actions. We turn, in fact, to insurance companies of every kind. In the sphere of the human community where we may have to face failure and loss of face, we resort to convention, social forms, habit. How impervious can we be to the temptation of ' insurance ' when we have to deal with the incalculable powers of the beyond? It is true that man might insure himself against other worldly powers, against God himself, by simply pretending that he no longer believes in these things. But who can deny that there is a subconscious world, a world full of mysteries which want to assert themselves and whose outspoken claim man ignores only to succumb to his own hidden insecurity? Is it not logical to assume that many of those who care nothing about the Church's message of salvation and its moral requirements still shrink from an open break with the Church and continue to attend its services, longing for the final ' insurance ' of the Church?

These are the two directions which current misunderstandings of the Church take. These errors naturally assume different forms for different people at different times. Still, almost all of man's speculations about the Church can be fitted under these two headings. The positive elements in these opinions are not false. The error lies much more in the fact that one thesis is isolated from the true synthesis and becomes false when put in opposition to an antithesis. The Church *is* a society whose realization depends on the free decisions of its members. The Church at the same time is *also* a 'collective unity,' which exists prior to the individual decisions, which permits the individuals to incorporate themselves in order to assure themselves of the blessings of afterlife. The life of the Church operates in various dimensions and combines them in a mutual interpenetration. Error lies in setting up one dimension against another.

THE CHURCH AS THREE-DIMENSIONAL REALITY

The existence of the Church reaches into three dimensions. This is not to be an abstract presentation of the nature of the Church. The history of theology shows that the mystery of the Church cannot be pinned down to an unequivocal abstract definition. Apart from all other difficulties, attempting an abstract definition of the essence of the Church runs the risk of overlooking its existential character. The Church is the historical setting of man's redemption by Jesus Christ. As such it cannot stay within the abstract sphere of essentiality but must be seen in the area of that reality in which redemption must be effected.

The Vertical Dimension

The first dimension which determines the existence of the Church is the vertical dimension. Here is found the real meaning and purpose of the work of the visible Church. This vertical dimension is actually what we call ' salvation ' and it is presented symbolically in the visible Church and is brought within the reach of men longing to be saved. This vertical aspect of the Church's existence brings us close to those allegorical phrases which the New Testament and the early Christian tradition use to speak about the nature of the Church.

There is, for instance, an image of the Church that is perhaps somewhat farfetched for us, but one the early Church had confidence in and which had already contributed to the self-understanding of the People of God of Old Testament times. This image pictures the Church as a bride ' whom Christ loved and for whom he delivered himself up that he might sanctify her, cleansing her in the bath of water by means of the word ' (*Eph.* 5: 25–6). Another image, much favoured by Paul, compares the Church to a body whose head, in the sense of chief, is Christ (in the main Pauline epistles), or as the body which the exalted Christ holds together and infuses with divine life that unites the many members into a living body (in the captivity epistles). As with Paul, so with Peter: he called the Church by the Old Testament designation, the People of God, a group separate from other men who not only are not God's people but are not a ' people ' at all. ' You who in times past were not a people, are now the people of God ' (1 *Pet.* 2: 10). In addition, the Church is called a temple of God or of the Holy Spirit. Finally, let us add the allegory which played a great part in the tradition of the Church Fathers: that of the Church as a Virgin Mother who permits Christians to partake of the divine life of salvation in her embrace.[3] This concept, too, can be found in the Scriptures. Paul shows the difference between the Old and the New Testament by comparing them to Abraham's sons, ' the one (born) by a slave-girl and the other by a free woman. And the son of the slave-girl was born according to the flesh, but the son of the free woman in virtue of the promise. This is said by way of allegory. For these are the two covenants: one indeed from Mount Sinai, bringing forth children unto bondage, which is Agar . . . But that Jerusalem which is above is free, which is our mother ' (*Gal.* 4: 22–6). John's second epistle is addressed to ' the Elect Lady and to her children whom I love in truth ' (2 *John* 1: 1), and the community receives greetings from ' the children of thy sister Elect ' (2 *John* 1: 13). Finally, the Church appears in the Apocalypse of John as the great portent in heaven, ' a woman clothed with

[3] See Hugo Rahner, S.J., *Mater Ecclesia.* Lopreis der Kirche aus dem ersten Jahrtausend Christlicher Literatur. Köln-Einsiedeln, 1944.

the sun, and the moon was under her feet, and upon her head a crown of twelve stars. And being with child . . . she brought forth a male child, who is to rule all nations with a rod of iron . . . and the dragon was angered at the woman, and went away to wage war with the rest of her offspring, who keep the commandments of God' (*Apoc.* 12: 1 ff.).

There are two significant things which concern us in these allegories. One is the polarity which is attributed to the Church. The Church lives in opposition to another reality which, when encountered, makes of it what it is supposed to be: a redeemed people of God. If the Church is a bride, we look for the bridegroom in whose encounter she will find her fulfilment. When this bride is called mother, we ask where the father is in the encounter wherein the Church becomes the mother of the believers. In the encounter with God the people of God becomes a Church. As a body, the Church is linked to a head with which it is united, but which it confronts at the same time. Finally, the Church becomes holy through the coming of the Holy Spirit, making it into a temple.

The other thing to note is that the polarity of encounter reaches upward, into the vertical dimension. The allegories we have mentioned proclaim the life of the Church in its strong dynamism between the Church on earth and the Lord in heaven. The Church recognizes the bridegroom as the glorified Lord in heaven. Her bridal love is longing to be with Christ, 'a lot by far the better' (*Phil.* 1: 23). God makes the Church his people to whom he reaches down from heaven to free from the bonds of the here and now. The head of the Church is the glorified Christ who vivifies the body of his Church through the Holy Spirit: 'He who cleaves to the Lord is one spirit with him' (1 *Cor.* 6: 17). 'One body and one Spirit, even as you were called in one hope of your calling' (*Eph.* 4: 4).

Thus the life of the Church stretches into the vertical dimension, between earth and heaven. The holy God communicates himself to the Church on earth and makes it holy. In the full strength of that life which is the Lord himself, the Church reaches into heaven, remembering the warning which Paul addressed to the Colossians: '. . . if you have risen with Christ, seek the things that are above, where Christ is seated at the right hand of God. Mind the things that are above, not the things that are on earth' (*Col.* 3: 1). And because the glorified Lord told of his second coming, the upward movement becomes the eschatological expectation of the future.

The Dimension of Depth

A second dimension in the life of the Church—that of depth—is sometimes in competition with the first, though it evolves by necessity from it. In the first dimension the Church, as a humble bride, longingly reaches towards her glorified Lord and receives life from him. This enables the Church to take the position of having something to give to the other sphere which we call the world. In the New Testament this notion has a contradictory meaning. The world is the sphere into which Christ sent the Church to fulfil a task there. At the same time ' the world ' stands for all the powers hostile to God. Hence the ambivalence of the relation of this dimension of ecclesial life with the first: on the one hand the Church confronts the world with tasks to do, since she has received her life from the glorified Lord to bring into the world; on the other hand her relations with the world are a constant danger to her union with the bridegroom in heaven.

Just as the Church, in her bridal encounter with Christ is the redeemed people of God, so the world, by its encounter with the Church which will penetrate its members, will be redeemed from the curse which is oppressing it. In the first dimension we saw the Church standing in a receiving position before Christ in heaven; the prototype here is the believing Mary who by her acceptance of the Annunciation received the Son of God sent into our history from on high. In the second dimension, by contrast, we see the Church in a giving position before the world. The world ceases to be simply profane, because the Church makes God present in it. It is not difficult to see an inner connection between the two dimensions. The fact that the Church has been ' called out ' to receive divine grace from the glorified Lord, does not simply separate it from the community of those from whom it was called out. On the contrary: the receiving of Christ means at the same time a mandate to pass on in salvific work in the arena of the world that which was received. In the community of salvation, as in the natural community, the act of giving does not simply end in the reception of the gift; the one receiving it is always inspired by it to give anew. The Church, before Christ a receptive bride, must also represent the bridegroom before the world which in a real sense it must woo.

This connection between receiving and giving in the first and second dimensions of ecclesial existence, is exemplified in the person of the Redeemer himself. After he stood receptively before God in eternal pre-existence, the God-man became the dispenser of divine life to a world in need of redemption. For the second Person of the Trinity is distinguished from the first in that he possesses the equal nature of divinity in the mode of *receiving*, while in the mode of giving it is proper to the Father. The Son of God, who received from the Father, was sent to become man so that he could now stand as a giver before men who were in need of redemption. These men, however, who stand facing him as a receiving Church are sent as givers: ' to the ends of the earth ' (*Matt.* 18: 28); ' As my father has sent me, so I send you ' (*John* 2: 21).

The Horizontal Dimension

In speaking of the Church as sign, we must pay special attention to the interpretation of the third dimension of the existence of the Church. If the first dimension reached up to heaven, and the second down, so to speak, into the depths, we may see the third as the horizontal dimension which includes the whole spectrum of the Church's social existence. Primitive Christianity was characterized by the first dimension—the desire for heaven and eschatological meaning—without denying or overlooking the second and third dimensions. In the Church of our day a special feeling for the social involvement of the Church has been awakened.

Today the visible, organized aspects of the Church engage our attention. We are inclined, as children of our times, to accept as real only that which is presented to our senses. But one who has experienced the reality of God in an encounter with him, can understand, in spite of criticism of the organized Church, that God is working his will of salvation within it, so that we may count upon him.

Scepticism and unbelief frequently start with criticism of the visible Church. It is no longer fashionable to deny the existence of a God and our indebtedness to him. Criticism of the Church, however, often finds ready listeners even among the faithful. We are unwilling to accept all the consequences for the Church, of God's decision to allow his Son to become man. It is a risk already prepared for in the Old Testament: to descend with his untouchable transcendence into human vulnerability, subject to man's criticism.

When one speaks of the Church, attention is usually focused on the hierarchy, the official Church. For those who criticize, this is very convenient. Members of the Church can criticize without themselves being implicated if they do not belong to the hierarchy. We cannot simply dismiss as wrong the habit of seeing the Church primarily in its horizontal social dimension. There is certainly a continual tension between this dimension and the first, or vertical, dimension of the Church's life. It is precisely against the danger of institutional stagnation that the same Lord who founded the institutional Church wakens those powers we call charismatic. These charisms should remind us constantly of the dynamic vertical encounter with the Lord of heaven. The horizontal dimension of existence as a community and institution must fit in as just one of the three dimensions, which only together can make a complete and authentic definition of the Church.

This definition of the Church is now our next question as we investigate the relationship of all three dimensions in the life of the Church—but particularly the relationship of the vertical to the horizontal. We answer the question by saying that the visible Church with its two complementary elements, clergy and laity, is the sign instituted by Christ himself of the vertical confrontation of that same Church with the glorified Lord in heaven.

THE CHURCH AS SACRAMENTAL SIGN

A Negative Statement

First, a negative statement: We must not use one dimension of the Church against another.

Church history has repeatedly shown how great the temptation is to take the dimensions of the Church which belong together as equals and contrast one to the other like the three dimensions of the physical world. This is hardly astonishing considering the nature of the thing.

Religious men, influenced by the mystery of their inner encounter with God, continually call upon the transcendental aspect of the Christian faith as an argument against the social and indeed even the earthly character of Church life. Religious encounter with Christ in the Holy Spirit seems to be much too interior to be supported by an organized society, even if it is called a Church. The bridal attitude before the glorified Lord seems to be so personal and individual a matter that it cannot be contained by a legal-juridical framework. Being spiritually moved by grace in the religious life in Christ seems to transcend and to eliminate the need for the kind of human initiative that is proper to an organization. Thus we always find the opposition between mysticism and institution; between the Church of love and the juridical Church. Canon Law is proclaimed to be contradictory to the hidden and genuine nature of the Church.

Mixed with this struggle of the vertical charismatic attitude and horizontal social life of the institutional Church is also the struggle of action in the world against both these two dimensions equally. The apostolic, missionary activity of the layman is sometimes misunderstood as competing with the function of the clergy. Thus the encounter of the Church with the world is mistaken as opposition between the clerical office and the laity. Or, the true awakening of the layman is confused with propagandizing activism and he is thereby exposed to the danger of neglecting the vertical dimension of a believing encounter with his heavenly Lord.

It is not surprising that the institutional Church seeks to defend itself against these dangers by trying to play off the juridical-social horizontal dimension of her existence against the charismatic vertical dimension and the missionary dimension of depth. We know that the foundations of the visible Church have been laid by Christ. We also know that he has permanently implanted in his Church, the two components—the official Church and the lay community. How natural it is to place trust in juridical security higher than trust in the Holy Spirit, whom the Church acknowledges as its soul.

Signs of Salvation

Although we can identify these different dimensions of the Church, they can only be experienced together, in their unity. The life of the Church seen as a visible hierarchical society has for its purpose the incarnation of the dimension of religious Christian life—a dimension so difficult to control because it is directed towards the other life—and guaranteeing it by a sacramental sign.

Being interpreted as a sign gives the visible Church, which often appears so obtrusive, a noteworthy ambivalence. And to have to give equal consideration to both aspects makes a true acknowledgment quite difficult. The ambivalence consists in the fact that the Church, because it must be considered a sign, is placed at the centre of our religious consideration; because a sign stands for something beyond itself. It is the nature of a sign to set both centripetal and centrifugal forces into motion at the same time. Thus the Church in its visible aspects inevitably attracts attention to itself. This does not sit well with those who cannot bear the idea of the incarnation of the holy God within a visible Church on earth.

Representatives of the Church may also allow to be forgotten what may not be forgotten: that the Church must attract attention to itself only because the encounter of the two complementary lives of priestly office and lay community symbolically represents the invisible encounter of redeemed man and the heavenly Redeemer. When Christ founded the Church and established the relationship between the apostles and their successors and the laity, he transferred, so to speak, the salvific vertical encounter with the glorified Christ onto the horizontal plane of the Church as a society. This does not mean a substitution of priest for Christ; redeemed man does not encounter the priest of the Church instead of the glorified Lord. This would be a poor substitute. What is meant is that the face-to-face meeting of priest and layman on earth should be a symbol of the confrontation of the risen Christ with his Church on earth and should keep the devotion to God from becoming too other-worldly at the expense of commitment to the here and now. Christ, who is in heaven, enters the visible realm of the Church in his official representatives who, in the words of John Chrysostom, ' lend him their tongues and offer their hands in his service,' and thus Christ encounters his community bodily, bringing graces.[4] For, ' we are Christ's ambassadors ' (2 *Cor.* 5: 20), Paul has said for all bearers of the ecclesiastical office. Since the Church as sign is constructed around two poles, it symbolizes an encounter. And since it is a sign of encounter, its content comes from both components: from man who as a member of the lay community comes to meet the

[4] St John Chrysostom, *Epistle*, 86: 4.

Lord, and from the Lord, represented by the ecclesiastical office. In one it is the mission which calls the members of the Church; in the other it is the guarantee that the Church as sacrament makes as a salvific sign.

For the layman who enters into relationship with the Church's teaching-, pastoral-, and priestly-offices, the symbolic character of the Church sounds a warning note. If it is true that to a certain degree his 'horizontal' encounter with the priestly office of the Church signifies a 'vertical' confrontation with the glorified Lord, he must be sure that this symbolic meeting is sincere, that is, his physical, external encounter with Christ's representative must testify to his personal, interior devotion to God and to Christ.

Thus that part of the Church's symbolic life which is directed to the Lord has this meaning: in the holder of ecclesiastical office Christ himself comes really and effectively in grace to members of the community. This is the profound meaning of the fact that the Church was founded by Christ. Not only does this fact guarantee the actual life of the Church to the end of time, but it also guarantees that in the Church the man who makes his relationship to the priest acting in an official capacity a sincere sign of his dedication to God, encounters in him the grace of Christ. When Christ instituted the Church he made a promise. God does what he promises, and what he promises to do through his Church, that he will also do.

The essential life functions by which the Church makes present the encounter with the glorified God and realizes his mediation will be discussed in the next two chapters.

Chapter Two

The Saving Action of the Church in Word and Sacrament

We have discussed the Church as a sacramental sign of salvation. We recognized that the Church was instituted by Christ as a society and therefore has all the marks of one. But the true nature of the Church and its basic function as a society can be understood only in the light of the symbolic purpose which gives all that is visible in the Church its profound meaning. This sign-characteristic is not simply a development of the Church as a visible society but is on the contrary a new reality. The Church, which above and beyond its organizational purpose has a symbolic meaning in relation to the divine, contains this distinctive divine quality so actively and effectively that whoever involves himself in the visible Church receives divine life through grace.

With this ' effective ' aspect of the Church as the sign of salvation, we have arrived at a point where the theme of this and the next chapter begins to take shape. What we looked at in the previous chapter showed the Church in its existential being which institution by Christ had given it. But in order to be efficacious it must *act*. If a sign or symbol is to be effective it cannot be an image made of dead lines which does no more than remind the observer of something which he then strives to do through his own power. If the image or sign itself is to be effective, it must itself be living and real.

This leads us from the static observation of the Church which we made in the preceding chapter, to the life function in which it is active. The two poles which Christ established—ecclesiastical office and lay community—are so interdependent that their dynamic relationship actualizes the life and saving action of the Church. If one really wants to know what the Church is, one must see it active in these life functions.

At first glance the life of the Church seems to be made up of a confusing variety of activities. However, perception sharpened by faith will clearly distinguish two different types of action in this multiplicity: the first includes those actions of the Church that follow from its teaching and pastoral office in the service of the proclamation of the word of God. To the second belongs the sacramental worship which the Church exercises by reason of its priestly office. It is these two topics which we will discuss in this chapter. The relationship between word and sacrament, as well as the Church service connected with each, can be examined from the different points of view: how does the spoken word differ from the visible sign, for instance, or in what way does the symbolic action of the sacraments make an essential contribution to the proclamation of the word in preaching, or many others. Of all these possible points of view, only one is pertinent to our overall theme: namely, how the symbolic presentation of salvation is realized in both areas of the life of the Church. In the first part we shall explain how and why the essential, life saving functions of the Church consist in the twofold action of word and sacrament. The second part will examine how the divine guarantee, which by virtue of the institution of the Church by Christ is given as a promise of God, operates in this twofold function.

WORD AND SACRAMENT AS REPRESENTATION OF THE SALVATION EVENT

Let us start with a comparison, which at first may not seem appropriate and yet may help clarify things. A person contemplates a picture by a modern artist—a somewhat objective work which permits the question, ' What does it actually represent? ' The at first perplexed viewer is told that in this picture a certain landscape is reproduced which he himself has seen in nature; or that a certain person is portrayed whom he himself knows. His perplexity then disappears. Now he is able to interpret the total conception and details of the picture, and he also perceives what is supposed to be expressed in this kind of picture, which at first had seemed so capricious.

What does this comparison mean in connection with our topic?

We have talked about the Church, with its contrast of ecclesiastical and lay functions, as a sign of the confrontation of Christ, the bridegroom and head, with the Church as bride and body. But we had a reason for saying ' sign ' instead of ' image.' The Church and its life functions portray what takes place between the risen Christ and the Church of the here-and-now, but not in the careful, detailed style of a naturalistic painting. The Church is a symbolic or sacramental image, a *sign* from which we can read the essential structure of the salvation-event, if and when we have been taught about this structure in faith. Just as the meaning of the picture in our example became clear as soon as one realized what it represented, so we explain the structure and shape of the Church's life by asking ourselves how this supernatural reality operates which is made present to us through the life functions of the visible Church, in order that we as physical men can incorporate ourselves in it.

The Fact of Redemption in Christ

What happens in the Church in the encounter between the pastoral office and the laity is a projection into human society of the actual salvific encounter between God and man whose ultimate consummation is in heaven. The redemptive event which takes place in Christ between God and men and which is echoed constantly by the Church, is represented and made effective when the two aspects of the life of the Church encounter each other in word and sacrament. We thus have to examine more closely how our redemption in Jesus Christ is effected. This will clarify for us the meaning and sense of the proclamation of the word and the sacramental worship of the Church.

How our redemption through Christ happens is clearly illustrated for us in the concept of the mediator, which characterizes Christ's role in God's plan of salvation according to the epistle to the Hebrews and the first epistle to Timothy: 'For there is one God, and one Mediator between God and men, himself man, Christ Jesus' (1 *Tim.* 2: 5), and 'he is mediator of a new covenant' (*Heb.* 9: 15). This concept presupposes that even before the mediator begins his activity, there are two parties involved. 'There is no mediator where there is only one,' said Paul in his letter to the Galatians (3: 20). At first the two poles are not only facing each other but are in opposition: God the Creator on one side, and on the other, mankind, which as creature is infinitely different from him and separated in enmity through sin. The one who is to be the mediator first stands entirely on the side of God—he is the second person of the Holy Trinity. The work of redemption begins when the Son of God is sent by the Father to enter into human history and become man. The Father sends his son as an indication of his reconciliation to sinful mankind. He is the Word which the Father addresses to sinfully hostile mankind in reconciliation. This movement in which God himself arrived in our midst is matched by a return movement of sacrifice, in which the same mediator, as head of the human race, carries back to the Father the response of man. In his incarnation Christ is God's word to men; as victim he is the answer of man to God. Redemption is a dialogue whose first phase is the mediating descent of the Son of God as the Word of the Father to men, and whose second phase is the ascent of this God-man to the Father in sacrifice.

The Presentation of Redemption in the Life of the Church

This ' Christ event ' is what is symbolized in the life of the Church as a sign of salvation. Thus the life of the Church, like that of Christ, is divided into two complementary functions, the service of the word and the service of sacrifice.

How can the incarnation of the Word of God, with its effect of revealing and delivering God to men, be better represented or made clearer than by the Church transmitting the Word of God in the form of the gospel message to all mankind? Here we must not understand the expression ' Word of God ' simply as an address or communication of a thought, as might be concluded from human conversation. The proclamation of the Word of God through the Church partakes of the communicative power of the divine word, which conveys in the incarnation not just knowledge, but actually brings an invisible God within the reach of mankind. It is really intended that every word that is spoken be a sharing of some part of the person who is speaking. This is actually fulfilled in the Word of God addressed to man, as it happens in the incarnation: God has put himself into human history. The proclamation of the word of God through the Church partakes of this dimension of reality. The words of the Lord to his apostles: 'As the Father has sent me, I also send you' (*John* 20: 21), could be paraphrased: 'As I, sent by the Father, have brought God himself to men, so you, sent by me, will bring me to men.' The relationship of the proclamation of the word of God by the Church to the incarnation of the Word of God was forcefully stated by Pope Pius XII: 'Preaching the word of God is a great mystery . . . There is a close relationship between the incarnation and the preaching of the word of God, a wonderful closeness and kinship. Like the Blessed Virgin Mary, the disciple of Christ presents Christ to man. He is a Christ-bearer. The Mother of God clothes his limbs, the preacher of the Gospel clothes him in words. The manner is different, but the effect is the same.' [1]

In the historic work of redemption, the incar-

[1] Acta Apostolica Sedis, 38 (1946) 388.

nation was completed by the sacrifice on the cross, as the word was completed by the answer. Thus in the life of the Church the celebration of the sacraments is an answer, in a sense, to the proclamation of the Word of God by the Church. What the Council of Trent declared concerning baptism is applicable to all the sacraments: it is a *sacramentum fidei*, which could be translated as 'symbolic expression of faith.' Precisely because we accept in faith the Word of God as proclaimed by the Church, our faith must lead us further to the reception of the sacraments in which the sacrifice of Christ is presented and completed. What is heard in faith is answered in sacrament. This intimate dialogue of proclamation of the Word of God and celebration of the sacraments is expressed clearly in the central liturgical celebration of the Church, the Holy Eucharist. In the Mass the sacrificial death of Christ is represented by the presence of bread and wine on the altar, as Pius XII said again in his liturgical encyclical *Mediator Dei* in 1947,[2] when he pointed out that the presence of Christ under the separate species of bread and wine indicated a symbolic reference to the division of flesh and blood in the sacrificial death. But to make it quite clear that this sacrifice of the God-man is the return gift for another gift

[2] Herder edition, ed. Leo Koep, No. 69.

which first came down to us from God—the Church has put the service of the word as a separate part of the Mass before the service of sacrifice. This means more than merely that we should be instructed and admonished first about what is happening in the mystery of the Eucharist, so that we will show the right attitude during the sacrifice. The readings and the preachings of the word of God, by their very occurrence during the celebration of the Mass (and not only through their content) are a symbolic sign that the sacrifice of Christ and the co-sacrifice of men do not come first, but rather are an answer to the self-revelation of God to men which precedes every human effort.

In order to avoid misconceptions we hasten to say that the above does not exclude the fact that the proclamation of the word of God also represents the sacrificial death of the Lord, and the eucharistic feast also represents the incarnation of the Word of God. Both the readings and the preaching speak of the redeeming sacrifice, for ' as often as you shall eat this bread and drink the cup, you proclaim the death of the Lord, until he comes ' (1 *Cor.* 11 : 26). This is self-evident if we consider the content of the two life functions which Church combines within herself. But when we contemplate the immediate meaning of what is happening in these parts of the Mass, we cannot deny that the proclamation of the Word of God mirrors and represents directly and above all the incarnation of the Word of God, whereas the sacramental sacrifice represents and mirrors directly and above all the sacrificial offering of the Lord. How the sacraments, co-ordinated to the celebration of the Eucharist, present the offering of Christ in the life of the Church will be treated in the next chapter.

The following considerations will attest to the fact that the sacraments as presentations of the sacrificial worship of Christ are acts whose immediate direction of meaning is *upward* and therefore correspond to the *descending* direction of the meaning of the proclamation of the word as an answer. According to the Council of Florence the sacraments are celebrated 'through the material action (*res*) as matter, through the word (*verbum*) as form.' [3] The determining factor in the celebration of the sacraments is again the word. At first glance we might consider the sacramental celebration equal to the event of the proclamation of the Word. Both seem to be directed in like manner from God to man. But this impression proves deceptive if one reflects on what kind of word it is which determines the form of the sacramental act. Then it is evident through the very

[3] Denzinger 695.

word, which is the soul of the sacramental sign, that the direction of meaning from below upward is confirmed. In the New Testament the word used by the Church in dispensing its sacraments, is always *proseuche*, that is, prayer. This prayer of the Church is directed upwards to God in union with the God-man. Thus do the apostles administer the sacrament of Confirmation upon the Samaritans: 'they prayed for them, that they might receive the Holy Spirit, for as yet he had not come down on any of them . . . Then they laid their hands on them and they received the Holy Spirit' (*Acts* 8: 15–17). The sacrament of anointing (extreme unction) is administered by the priest anointing the sick 'with oil in the name of the Lord. And the prayer of faith will save the sick man' (*James* 5: 14). The deacons are consecrated by the apostles who after they had prayed 'laid their hands upon them' (*Acts* 6: 6). The words of consecration of the sacrament of the Eucharist have themselves the same unconditional form of the words Christ used in instituting the sacrament. But the sacrificing Christ who says them does indeed to that extent stand here below as he ascends from our midst to the Father in sacrifice. In very early times the Church added to the words of the consecration by an '*epiclesis*' which surrounded it as a petitioning prayer of the Church.

Thus the word which gives meaning and effectiveness to the sacramental sign is not issued as the word of proclamation of God to men, but ascends to God from below as the prayer of the Church in Christ the victim.

The two basic life functions of the Church represent therefore, the work of the Mediator in his two phases—the descent to us in the incarnation of the Word, and the ascent to God in sacrifice for mankind. Around these two essential functions—proclamation of the word of God and celebration of the sacraments—everything else the Church does by reason of her office are grouped, as satellites around the sun. Everything the Church does either emanates from these two essential functions, or it is not a proper work of the Church. Thus representatives of the Church quite rightly make frequent comments in the areas of politics, the natural sciences, technology, medicine, and sociology. Although these belong to the profane sphere they often contain points of view which make them a part of Church concern. All teaching done in these areas by the Church is understood to be an emanation of the incarnation of the divine Word—and thus derived from the service of the word of God. Charitable activity, whether organized or done through individual initiative, is an example of a service done for a neighbour which in reality is an emanation from the sacramental worship dimension of Church life. The New Testament, as we know, leaves no doubt that giving to God must be realized in giving to neighbour. But it is not possible in this space to examine this relationship more closely.

THE SAVING POWER OF THE LIFE FUNCTIONS OF THE CHURCH

What must be discussed now is that guarantee of an infallible efficacy which is characteristic of the life functions of the Church and which results from the institution of the Church by Jesus Christ. This guarantee makes the sign an efficacious instrument of our salvation.

Meaningful Signs

This divine guarantee signifies that the life functions of the Church are instruments for the attainment of our salvation, but at the same time are *sign*, *symbol*, and *image* of our salvation. Only when man hears the call which they contain, does this sign have an effect on him. The life functions of the Church are completed by two partners who encounter each other in this sign: the priest who proclaims the word of God represents the Lord as he communicates with man; and in administering the sacrament he represents Christ as he includes man in his sacrifice and brings it to the Father. But the believer who hears the word of God and receives the sacrament thereby acknowledges his need for salvation.

The guarantee of infallible efficacy has a double aspect, not in regard to the effectiveness, but in regard to its actual application. The guaranteed efficacy is nothing but the content which the sign is supposed to have. The hand which is stretched out in a gesture of encounter leads to a real meeting only when it can be put into the hand of the person encountered. The guarantee inherent in the Church is that fidelity with which God gives the promised meaning to the Christ-instituted sacraments wherever they are validly administered provided the faithful make their receiving of these sacraments a sincere expression of their return offering to God. We shall say more about these two interior factors which give the life functions of the Church their saving content: the divine faithfulness and the human acknowledgement of the need for salvation which should lead to drinking in the word of God and eagerly grasping the sacrament of Christ.

The Divine Guarantee

As far as the seven sacraments are concerned, we are familiar with their divine guarantee of efficacy. Following the Reformation controversies over this question, the Council of Trent solemnly proclaimed that the sacraments impart '*ex opere operato*' the grace which they symbolize. Thus the simple performance of the sacramental sign assures the imparting of grace. This has been taught to every Catholic from early childhood and is taken for granted as part of our religious consciousness. So we may have difficulty in dealing with the criticism of our sacramental faith by others which, once heard, easily finds an echo in our own hearts . . . You are trying to master through charms and magic what is freely given as a gift, that is, grace.

This objection can only be met if we keep in mind what we have explained before: The life functions of the Church are signs of a personal and reciprocal offering of God and man—the giver and the receiver of the sacraments. Only thus is the reception of grace assured, because God cannot withhold meaning from something which he himself instituted; he would then be untrue to himself. Holy Scripture, the Old and the New Testament alike, are filled with assurances that God is faithful and that the covenant he made with man will never be broken. Would it not be reasonable therefore that as evidence of his steadfast faithfulness to his covenant, he give a sign instituted once and for all time, as we believe the sacramental salvation-signs of the Church to be? In their individual celebrations these signs indicate that the sacrifice of Christ is repeatedly placed at the disposal of men here and now; God therefore is also prepared to give himself as the fruit of Christ's sacrifice to men. But the fact that the sacraments are instituted by Christ, for all time, is also a sign. It signifies the lasting faithfulness of God to the covenant, which is made present and efficacious through the action of the Church.

This is the divine guarantee which is inherent in the seven sacraments. But the proclamation of the word of God in the Church is also a symbolic presentation of an essential part of the event of salvation. As familiar as we are with the truth that the seven sacraments actually impart grace, it may arouse astonishment to hear that the proclamation by the Church of the word of God also contains the divine guarantee of efficacy. It is true, we do know of one guarantee: whenever the Church uses its authority to proclaim a truth revealed by God—whenever it acts in its highest teaching authority through the bishops of the world who unanimously proclaim the word of God, united with the pope as the highest authority of the Church—Christ himself has promised that the Holy Spirit will keep it from error and will promote the true understanding of his revelation. But how rarely do we encounter this solemn proclamation of the truth of God! Occasionally where the Church is proclaiming something God is more hidden than revealed by the person of the preacher.

Again we must consider what we have already said earlier: The proclamation by the Church of the word of God does not serve our salvation only by giving understanding to our intellects and activating our wills. The act of proclaiming itself, the act of preaching, is a symbolic presentation of the incarnation of the Word of God in Jesus Christ. But in the incarnation of Jesus Christ we were not only given knowledge and admonition. What happened there was the prototype of all grace: God communicated himself to man, entered into his history—into the history of mankind by the incarnation of Jesus Christ, into the history of each individual man through grace. Why, then, should the proclamation of the word of God by the Church not partake in the same way of the real content of incarnation as the sacraments do in imparting the efficacy of Christ's sacrifice? Put in a different way: Should not the divine guarantee which stands behind the preaching of the word of God in the Church consist in the fact that, in addition to imparting truth for our intelligence and dynamism for our will, it gives to us men the actual sharing in God himself which we call grace?

In the New Testament the same creative power which is inherent in the word of God all through Scripture, is ascribed also to the form in which the word of God is proclaimed to us in the Church. It is called the word of life: '. . . holding fast the word of life to my glory against the day of Christ; because not in vain have I run, neither in vain have I laboured' (*Phil.* 2: 16). It is the word of grace: '[Paul and Barnabas] . . . gave testimony to the word of his grace by permitting signs and wonders to be performed by their hands' (*Acts* 14: 3). And in taking leave, St Paul tells the presbyters of Ephesus: 'Now I commend you to God, and to the word of his grace' (*Acts* 20: 32). The proclamation of the Church is the word of reconciliation instituted by God: 'For God was truly in Christ, reconciling the world to himself . . . by entrusting to us the message of reconciliation' (2 *Cor.* 5: 19). This means not only that the word that is proclaimed speaks of life, grace, and reconciliation, but that the proclamation *contains* life, grace, and reconciliation and has its effect on those who hear it.[4] Thus the priest prays after the gospel at Mass that its words may take away sin. At the consecration of deacon and subdeacon, according to the Roman Pontifical, they are empowered to read the epistle and the gospel 'for the living and the dead.' It brings salvation even to those who have died, whose understanding can no longer be enriched by the word of God, and whose disposition of will can no longer be changed. This can mean only some kind of objective imparting of grace which is exercised through the proclamation of the word of God by the Church. Therefore there is obviously an assurance of grace in the proclamation of the word by the Church in which the incarnation of the Word of God is represented symbolically. As with the sacraments, this efficacy of the proclamation of the word of God is independent of the personal attitude of the preacher. For this Paul is an impressive witness, when he reports to the Philippians that 'Some indeed preach Christ even out of envy and contentiousness, but some also out of goodwill . . . But what of it? Provided only that in every way, whether in pretence or in truth, Christ is being proclaimed' (*Phil.* 1 : 15–18). Thus Pius XII characterized the relationship between

[4] Cf. R. Schlier, *The Word of God*. (Rothenfelser Reihe No. 4), Wurzburg, 1958. Karl Herman Schelkle, 'Das Wort in der Kirche' in *Theol. Quartalschrift* 133 (1933), 278–93.

incarnation and preaching by saying: 'The way and manner (of the Word of God coming to man) varies, but the effect is the same.'

Thus the preaching of the word of God is similar to the sacraments. The same elements which are inherent in the sacraments seem to be present here too: action which can be perceived by the senses, symbolizing a saving reality; the institution by Christ which is testified to in the words of Paul: 'God was truly in Christ . . . entrusting to us the message of reconciliation' (2 *Cor.* 5: 19);[5] and, finally, effectiveness for salvation. But this does not mean that preaching is the eighth sacrament and has its own saving effect along with the sacraments. This would run counter to the teachings of the Council of Trent.[6] Preaching and administering the sacraments are united in a dialogue, they are two elements of a complex event the whole of which is the source of grace. Thus the wellspring of all grace, the redeeming work of Christ, is composed of two elements: incarnation and sacrifice; word and response; offering of God to men and of men to God. The sacraments as the immediate representation of Christ's

[5] Cf. H. Schlier, 'Die Stiftung des Wortes Gottes nach dem Apostel Paulus,' *Theologie und Predigt*. Wurzburg, 1958.

[6] The Council of Trent taught in the introduction to the seventh session (Denzinger 843a; Neuner-Roos, *Der Glaube der Kirche in den Urkunden der Lehrverkundigung*, No. 412) that 'every true justice starts with the sacraments, grows or is recovered after a loss.'

sacrifice are salvific because they also contain the word which sounded in the proclamation of the Church. And the proclamation of the word of God as the immediate representation of the incarnation can be called salvific because it is directed towards and leads to the reception of the sacraments.[7]

Man's Disposition

If the proclamation of the word and the administering of the sacraments by the Church are symbolic signs of the grace dispensed through them, the performance of these signs makes an urgent appeal to man's disposition. He can be sure that God will fulfil what he promised by instituting these signs. But man himself must confirm the meaning of these signs which are demands on man as much as promises. First of all it is necessary that man enter into the sign as he receives them. Then, too, he must permit his disposition to be moulded by the content and meaning of the signs. The signs must be true, agreeing in expression and in content. Therefore man must understand the meaning which Christ intended in endowing the Church with the salvation signs. And he must take care to bring his personal disposition into

[7] On this subject see Otto Semmelroth, S.J., *The Preaching Word*, New York, 1965.

agreement with this intention. What does this mean for the individual?

First let us examine the way in which we are accustomed to accept the proclamation of the word of God. What do we expect from a sermon? Despite countless disappointments, we hope for a rewarding, well-developed theme. We actually do not bring a personal readiness to receive the word through the sermon, but rather want to be awakened by the form and content of the preaching. We want the sermon to stimulate us. This is a reasonable desire, but it is not all we should expect from a sermon. Not every sermon, after all, can affect us in this way. Rare are those preachers who are able to present the eternal truths without boring us and who are able to awaken in us a latent receptiveness.

Obviously, since the sermon concerns the word of God, it should be proclaimed as something said by God, both in content and manner of presentation. There is no encounter between persons without the word of one communicating something about himself to the other. But as much as the content of the proclamation of the word of God by the Church testifies to the self-revelation of God, preaching in itself is a symbolic act even without considering content. The fact that it is proclaimed, in the name of the Lord, points symbolically to the fundamental event of our redemption: that God's personal word was incarnate in Jesus Christ. The symbolic character of preaching is not of course entirely independent of the content and form of the sermon, but it exists and is effective even in a weak and poorly organized sermon. It is the charism of that salvation sign that the priestly representative of the Incarnate Word makes the listening members of the Church hear the word of God.

From this it follows that the listener has a new role. He cannot come as a dilettante looking forward to a well-presented and interesting content, but who closes up—switches off, as we say—when his expectations are not fulfilled. This would mean that he expected the body of the sermon without the soul—certainly without the divine soul which vitalizes even a dull sermon. The believing listener must take upon himself the role of collaborator in the symbolic act which the event of preaching represents. What is symbolized in preaching—the incarnation of the Word of God—needs for its realization the readiness to hear and believe of Mary, who thereby became the prototype of redemption.[8] Thus, both in the preaching itself through the proclaiming words of the preacher,

[8] Cf. Otto Semmelroth, S.J., *Mary, Archetype of the Church*, New York and Dublin, 1963.

and in the receiving of the word of God with the faith of Mary, through a readiness to listen, must the coming of the word of God in the incarnation be represented. It might be that this readiness to listen will be disappointed by the content and form of the preaching, but it will always retain its importance as a symbolic expression of the readiness to accept God in our own hearts through the grace which God communicates. Whenever a salvation sign guaranteed by God encounters this readiness, God's grace is assured.

Our participation in the sacraments also needs to be corrected, but in just the opposite way from our listening to preaching. We have long been accustomed to consider only the action by which the sacrament is administered as important, and to pay little attention to the content and the meaning of what is happening. It is like the act of driving a nail; it does not seem important what shape the instrument takes with which the action is to be effected. We have been too onesided in treating the sacramental action as an instrument through which grace becomes operative. That is the reason we really have no answer to the question of why there is not one but seven sacraments, all looking very different. We must remember that the sacraments are also signs; we must ask ourselves what is in these signs that is directed towards us and demands a response.

What is represented in these signs by virtue of Christ's purpose in instituting them and which therefore determines our disposition, is the sacrifice of Christ. Man enters into the sacrifice when he receives a sacrament and can be brought by it to God, if he so chooses. That which is represented and is contained in the sacramental symbolic action of the sacrifice of Christ is the guarantee that God's grace is given. But only by assuming the personal disposition, which was determined by the sacrificial Christ before the Father, can man guarantee that the pledge of Christ's sacrifice will be effective.

Thus the faithful enter the redemptive dialogue by listening to the word of proclamation by the Church and by receiving the sacramental action which Christ mediates by coming down to us as the Word of God and ascending to God as the offering of men. The symbolic presentation of this dialogue in the Church's worship of word and sacrament offers us this physical and divinely animated dialogue so that we ourselves may take part in it.

Chapter Three

The Seven Sacraments

In the seventh book of the second part of *Poetry and Truth*, Goethe has made some astonishing remarks about the sacraments of the Catholic Church. What he says is not, of course, the real mystery of Catholic belief in sacraments. His statements, however, take on a much deeper and richer meaning in the reality instituted by Christ than he could have ever imagined. From the Catholic point of view, is it not true that the sacraments are ' the high point of religion, the visible symbol of an extraordinary divine favour and grace '? The whole text is as follows: ' In things ethical and religious, as well as in those physical and civic, man does not like to act extemporaneously; he needs a sequence on which habit can be based. That which he should love and do, he cannot think of alone and isolated; in order to want to repeat something, it must not have become strange to him . . . The sacraments are the high point of a religion, the visible symbol of an extraordinary divine favour and grace . . . Such a sacrament may not stand alone. No Christian can enjoy it with real joy for which it is given, unless the symbolic or sacramental sense has been nourished in him. He must be accustomed to see the interior religion of the heart and the external religion of the Church as one complete unity, as a great common sacrament that can be divided into many different parts, each of which gives its own holiness, indestructibility and immortality.

'Here a young couple is joining hands, but not in a passing greeting, nor for a dance: the priest speaks his blessing over them, and the tie is indissoluble. In due time these marriage partners bring an offspring to the threshold of the altar; it is cleansed with holy water and incorporated into the Church in such a way that it can forfeit this benefit only by a monstrous apostasy. The child becomes increasingly skilled in earthly things; in those of heaven he must be instructed. If a test proves that he has been instructed, he is now accepted into the bosom of the Church as a true citizen, as a real and free believer, not without external signs of the importance of this action. Only now is he a committed Christian, only now does he recognize not only the privileges, but also the responsibilities. But in the meantime he, as a man, has encountered much that is wonderful; through instruction and punishment he has realized the sorry state of his interior life and still there will be talk of instructions and trespasses; but there should be no more punishment. Here, in the infinite confusion in which he is entangled through the contest between natural and religious demands, a marvellous means is given to him so that he can confide his deeds and misdeeds, his faults and his doubts, to a man who has been appointed for this very purpose, who knows how to comfort him, to warn him, to strengthen him, to punish through symbolic penance, and finally to render him happy by extinguishing his guilt completely and to return to him the slate of his humanity washed clean. Thus, prepared and reassured by several sacramental actions which, when examined closely, branch into several smaller sacramental rites, he kneels down to receive the sacred host; and so that the mystery of this holy act be still increased, he only sees the chalice from afar; it is not ordinary eating and drinking which satisfies; it is a heavenly meal which makes us thirst after the divine drink.

'But the youth must not think that this is all there is, not even the man must believe it. In earthly circumstances, it is true, we get accustomed to rely upon ourselves, and here also knowledge, understanding and character are not always sufficient. In heavenly things, however, we never finish learning. The higher feeling in us which often does not find itself at home, is being beset by so many external circumstances, that our own capacity hardly suffices to provide for everything which is necessary to give comfort, counsel and help. Prescribed for that purpose, however, is a medicine for the whole life and an understanding and devout man is continually waiting to lead those gone astray back to the right path and to help those that are tormented.

'What has thus been tested all through life, will now be proved in all its efficacy at the threshold of death. After a lifetime of amicable and trusting habits the declining man accepts with ardour those significant and symbolic assurances and is given divine guarantees for a beatific existence in all eternity where earthly guarantees have disappeared completely. He is convinced that neither a hostile element nor a disagreeable spirit can hinder him from being surrounded by a glorified body so that in direct relation to the Godhead he partakes in the immeasurable blessedness which flows from it.

'In the end, in order that the whole man be sanctified, even the feet are to be anointed and blessed. They should feel a reluctance to tread the hard, impenetrable earth in the event the patient recovered. They should be infused with a wonderful elasticity so that they repel the earth which until now had attracted them. And thus, cradle and grave, as far apart as they may be, are connected in a constant circle by a succession of equally sacred actions whose beauty has only been hinted at by us.

'But these spiritual wonders do not spring from the natural soil as other fruits do; they cannot be sowed, nor planted nor cultivated. They are to be conjured from another region, something that not everybody at every time succeeds in doing. Here we are faced with the oldest of the symbols from ancient tradition. We hear that one man can be distinguished above another by being blessed and sanctified from above. In order that this does not appear as a natural gift, this magnificent grace, which is tied to grave duties, must be passed from one who is empowered to another. This greatest good that man can obtain, without being able to receive it out of himself or striving after it, can be maintained and eternalized only through spiritual inheritance. In priestly consecration everything is summed up which is necessary to effect these sacred actions, without any other activity being necessary except belief and unconditional confidence. Thus the priest takes his place in the line of his predecessors and successors in the circle of the ordained, representing the highest blessing. He is the more elevated since it is not his person which we worship but his office, not his command, in front of which we kneel, but the blessing which he imparts and which is the more sacred, seemingly coming directly from heaven, because the human tool cannot weaken it, nor lose its power, no matter how sinful and even corrupted the human instrument might be.'

Not for the reason of easy apologetics or propagandizing did we begin this chapter with a quotation from Goethe, that non-Catholic Olympian, as an 'impartial' witness for the riches of our faith. The significance which the poet by his own admission discerned in our seven sacraments is important for the theme of this chapter, that is, that the presence of a controlling design in all multiformity of the seven sacraments should represent the cosmos. It is this unity within diversity, inherent in everything living, that so impressed Goethe. What man 'should love and do he he cannot think of as alone and isolated.' At the same time he makes a profound observation: how the ambivalence inherent in a holy God—of distance and nearness, of unapproachability and communication—is made clear in the symbol: 'The great, holy action (of the sacrament) in reality takes the place of the possible or the impossible, the place of that which man never can obtain nor do without.'

In the preceding chapter we were able to trace back the two elements in the life functions of the Church—the service of the word and the service of the sacrament—to the dialogue character of Christ's work of salvation. Now the question presents itself: where to look for the origin of the seven-sided form of the sacramental worship of the Church. What the God-man planted into his Church is also realized through him; John calls him the Logos, and the Logos determines the divine plan of salvation and shapes the essential characteristics of the existence of the Church. Three steps must be taken here. First we shall speak of the eucharistic celebration which is the focal point of the sacraments. The second part will show how the other sacraments draw in, consecrate and order our whole life in the celebration of the eucharistic sacrifice. In the third part we shall look at the 'fundamental sacrament'—the Church itself; for the foregoing considerations will show that through the sacraments a new relationship to the Church is established, and thereby a new bond of grace with God.

THE EUCHARISTIC SACRIFICE AS FOCAL POINT

When we say that the eucharistic celebration—the sacramental presentation of Christ's sacrifice—is the focal point of the sacramental cosmos, this has a twofold meaning: the Holy Eucharist is the centre of the Church, and therefore is also the heart of our human existence.

The Eucharist as the Centre of the Church

'The celebration of the Eucharist is the most intensive event of the Church. For in this celebration not only is Christ present in the worshipping action of the Church as the redeemer of his body and as Saviour and Lord of the Church, but in the Eucharist the unity of the faithful with Christ and with one another becomes most visible and is realized most deeply in the eucharistic meal. Inasmuch as the eucharistic celebration is also the sacramental anticipation of the eternal wedding feast in heaven, in this worshipping celebration also shines the final eternal form of the salvation community, so in it the wellspring of the Church, the sacrifice of Christ on the cross, is sacramentally present.' [1]

[1] Karl Rahner, S.J., *Mission and Grace*, London 1963, *The Christian Commitment*, New York, 1964.

The eucharistic celebration does not only stand in the physical centre of the various expressions of the life of the Church. It is itself the most intensive realization of what the institution of the Church, founded by Christ, signifies actually and potentially. We shall not demonstrate here by full historical documentation that the Church in all ages has considered the sacramental eucharistic celebration its focal point. Rather, two thoughts representing much testimony are submitted, one positive and the other negative.

The positive testimony is this: Paul used the relationship between man and wife in their marriage to describe the nature of the Church (*Eph.* 5: 21–33). It is remarkable what realistic power Paul ascribes to the symbolic relationship between the bond of man and wife in marriage, on one hand, and the bond of Christ and Church in the order of grace, on the other. From it he draws out very real consequences for the moral attitude of man and wife to each other. This can only come about through confidence in the grace-effecting power of the sacramental symbol, which is matrimony.

The Church is, therefore, described as that bridal community of people, redeemed by Christ, in that he has, by his death on the cross, offered, purified and prepared this community as his bride, 'without spot or wrinkle.' So, as the Church Fathers are fond of saying, the Church is the new Eve, sprung from the side of the second Adam, when he expired on the cross. Nowhere is this origin, so characteristic of the nature of the Church, more clearly or profoundly realized than in the celebration of the sacramental sacrifice of the Eucharist. Here the bridegroom is Christ, visibly present before the bridal community and present in the consummation of the sacrifice of the cross. For in the eucharistic celebration Christ is present under two forms: in the person of the celebrant, as a bridegroom before the bridal community; and under the species of bread and wine, as the offering which he presents to the Father for his Church, as a bridal present which he confers on the Church. Through his consecrating action with the two separate forms of the bread and wine the priest makes present the event of the offering, into which the community enters, as a bride, in a personal participation that achieves its complete and valid expression in the receiving of Holy Communion. Nowhere then can the nature of the Church be more intensively actualized than in the eucharistic celebration. Here the Church realizes itself most profoundly: when it celebrates its own inception from the side of Christ dying on the cross and anticipates the final bridal union by means of the eucharistic meal and sacrifice.

This can be established by examining a more negative testimony of the life of the Church, which will serve as a kind of cross-check. It is sacramental penance, practiced by the Church by virtue of Christ's institution. The early Christian manner of performing penance showed clearly what is also discernible today, that the penitential action is directed towards the Eucharist, the centre of the life of the Church. When a man in sin separates himself from a living community with God, the Church makes this visible by not allowing him to take part in the innermost life of the Church, the celebration of the Eucharist. In early Christianity this was done by a special edict of exclusion and demotion to the level of penitent. This completely excluded participation in the celebration of the Holy Eucharist. But even today, this making visible of the separation from God by separation in the Church is still achieved by prohibiting the sinner from taking part in the true and full sense in the eucharistic celebration: he is not allowed to receive Holy Communion. The forgiveness of sins through the sacrament of penance is accomplished first by the Church's re-admitting the sinner into its own fellowship and that means the possibility of participating in Holy

Communion. Peace with the Church is the pledge of restored communion with God. Thus the Lord's word about the sacrament of penance can rightly be interpreted: 'When you (that is, the Church) forgive the sins (insofar as they are an offence against the Church) of men (by accepting them again into your eucharistic community), they (that is, the sins, insofar as they are a separation from God) are forgiven (which means being raised up in a new living community with God)' (see *John* 20:23). We must never overlook how identical the 'peace with the Church' is with the ability to take part in the eucharistic celebration through reception of Holy Communion. Which proves that the Church knows itself to be realized in the Eucharist; that the Eucharist is the centre of its life!

The Eucharist as Centre of Human Life

But the Eucharist as sacramental enactment of the sacrifice of Christ has also moved into the centre of human existence. Since this is so, the Church, whose centre of life and most profound self-realization is the eucharistic sacrifice, is not just on the margin of life, which we need to leave behind in our daily affairs. Just as Pope Pius XII once called the Church 'the life principle of human society,' [2] so in the life of individual man the Church is the sanctifying principle of his existence in the world. There remains, to be sure, a difference between Church and world in our lives. And at certain times we embody the world more clearly in our life; at other times more expressly the Church. But actually, we are being determined by both. Church and world interpenetrate each other in our lives. Even in its worldly manifestations our life is valid only when it is permeated by our membership in the Church. In the first epistle of Peter (2 : 10), we find a striking alternative which is quite revealing. Peter appeals to the self-consciousness of Christians as 'people of God.' What he presents to them as an alternative to the 'people of God' is not a 'people of the devil' or 'people of the world.' Rather he says: 'You who in times past were not a people; but are now the people of God.' Therefore when it ceases to be the 'people of God,' and that is the Church, it ceases to be a people at all. So the alternative to a life that is permeated by the Church is not simply a life without the Church—but still a life. No, when the formation of life by the Church ceases, life itself loses its validity before God. And what other validity is there?

[2] Address to the new cardinals, Feb. 20, 1946, AAS 38 (1946) 149.

If belonging to the Church permeates our lives as a validating principle, and the centre of the Church is the eucharistic-sacramental celebration of Christ's sacrifice, then the co-celebration of Christ's sacrifice stands in the centre of our lives. A life of service in the material world and in the human environment must be continually orientated to the sacrificing service of Christ before the infinite God; and the sacrificial offering to God, so intensively celebrated in the Eucharist, must continually be acted out in the service of the world of creation and of men. The two might differ from one another according to the time and circumstances. But in the living unity of the faithful both interpenetrate each other.

This ordering of human life in all its dimension around the eucharistic centre is now made complete by the cosmos of the other sacraments.

THE OTHER SACRAMENTS AS CONSECRATION OF OUR LIVES

With the eucharistic celebration at the centre, the other six sacraments fall into two groups. One group makes the eucharistic life of the Church possible, while the other sanctifies human existence in its entirety in relation to this sacrifice.

Consecration of the Worshippers

Three consecrating sacraments and one that restores belong to the first group. The three consecrating sacraments are distinguished from the others by the nature of their effect. We know from the catechism lessons of our childhood that through baptism, confirmation and holy orders 'a mark is impressed upon the soul, that is, an indelible spiritual sign, so that they cannot be repeated.' [3] But who knows how to explain the meaning of this fact and above all to make clear how this indelible sign, given through baptism, confirmation and holy orders, is able to produce grace?

The indelible sign of baptism, confirmation and holy orders has a twofold meaning which in reality are two aspects of the same thing. First, through the sign that these sacraments impart, man is initially incorporated as a member of the mystical body of Christ, which is the Church, through baptism. Or he is given a definite place in this Church: adult responsibility in the work of the people of God, through confirmation; or an official role as representative of Christ, the head of the body, the bridegroom of his bride, through the sacramental seal of holy orders.

The institutional, Church-centred effect of

[3] Council of Trent, 7th Session, Denzinger 852.

these sacraments has at the same time a eucharistic aspect. The Church shows itself as the worshipping community gathered around the altar of the eucharistic sacrifice. Even when it is not actually assembled at Mass, it is the Church's nature to be a community which realizes and actualizes itself in the sacramental completion of the event from which it sprang. So it is logical that the same indelible mark that incorporated into the Church—into its lay community or the spiritual office representing Christ—what Thomas Aquinas and more recently Pius XII in his encyclical *Mediator Dei* [4] called a *deputation ad cultum christianum*, a mission and capacity for Christian worship, also produced this mission and capacity. Incorporation into the Church means to be prepared and qualified to celebrate the *cultus christianus*, as a priest making sacramentally present the sacrifice of Christ, in Christ's stead, or actively participating as a member of the redeemed people of God. Conversely, one is enabled to participate in Christ's sacrifice only by being qualified to participate in the ecclesial structure of the sacrifice—that is, in the celebration of the Holy Eucharist. This means being accepted into the Church whose exclusive property is this sacrifice. Baptism and confirmation furnish co-celebrants who gather around the altar

[4] Ed. by J. Herder, New York, No. 87, C.T.S., London 1947.

of the Lord. Holy orders call authorized representatives from their midst to the altar of the sacrificing Christ.

By reason of this ordering in the celebration or co-celebration of the sacramental sacrifice of Christ, baptism, confirmation and holy orders give us in addition to the indelible sign, the grace-charged community of life with God, which has its origin in Christ's sacrifice.

Here we must add immediately the sacrament of penance which shares with baptism the effect of the remission of sins. Baptism is the first and fundamental sacrament of the remission of sins, and at the same time its specific effect is acceptance into the Church and the call to the eucharistic-sacramental sacrifice. This combination shows without doubt that sin—though it occurs in the Church—is contrary to the nature of the Church. The Church possesses a dynamism to be ' without spot and wrinkle,' and therefore against sin. That of course is only the reverse side of the fact that the Church realizes itself most intimately in the sacramental celebration of Christ's sacrifice. Sacrifice means dedication to God in recognition of his majesty and glory. Sin, however, means a rejection of God, a revolt against his authority. Wherever a member of the Church sins, he acts against the meaning which is impressed upon him through the indelible mark of baptism, confirmation and holy orders. He can, of course, never lose this mark and the meaning that goes with it through sin. But the sinner can no longer make effective use of it unless he has submitted to the sacrament of penance. This penance cannot be sufficiently effected within the invisible sphere of man's interior life. It must be made visible in the Church, because sin is trespassing against the meaning and nature of the Church.

Therefore Christ has instituted in his Church the sacrament of penance to liberate from the effects of sin what is given originally through the signs of baptism, confirmation and holy orders. This liberation affords future possibility of spiritual growth.

The Entire Human Existence

Two sacraments remain which we must consider and examine in their relation to the eucharistic celebration: marriage and extreme unction. With these it is not so much a question as to why there are still two more, but rather why there are *only* two more. The answer is not entirely that the seven sacraments fit into the different situations of natural human existence, as was asserted in Goethe's text quoted earlier. Some theologians have also held this, and not without justification.

But there might well be other situations besides getting born, becoming adult, needing nourishment, entering into community obligations or marriage, becoming sick and dying, which would perhaps be worthy of special distinction through a sacrament. The real reason why there are just these two additional sacraments and no more must go a little deeper than simply the harmonizing of grace-life with the rhythm of natural human life.

The sacraments discussed so far have demonstrated the living relationship between celebrant and the people who co-offer within which the eucharistic ceremony can be celebrated, and which is strengthened and renewed in confession; marriage and extreme unction seem to indicate how much the entire human life in its two essential spheres of action, individuality and community, are to be redeemed and sanctified by Christ's sacrifice. What constantly threatens the wholeness and unity of our lives is that our unity is the product of various dualities which are not easy to integrate into a whole. Above all it is the duality of the individual and community, of being for one's self and being intent on community with others, which tempts us into a false either-or. When the sacraments with their sanctifying effect combine with their healing and wholemaking effect, their power will help to integrate the duality into a living unity. The eucharistic celebration is quite obviously at the same time the community action of the Church—what is being offered is the whole Christ, head and members—and the personal commitment of the individual—what is more individualistic than the sacrificial offering of self to God? Do not these two sacraments of matrimony and extreme unction stand at two points of human existence where they are evidence of a special consecration to the eucharistic sacrifice—consecration of human individuality in one case and of community in the other? Marriage is the seed of the human community which grows into the family. If it is consecrated as a sacrament, the human urge for community is itself consecrated. Man's individual existence-for-self, on the other hand, can hardly be more profoundly or more clearly realized than in the situation where he must really stand quite alone—in death. In the sacramental consecration during fatal illness, therefore, man in his individuality is consecrated in the sacrifice of Christ, which indeed he will co-offer in the highest possible imitation through his own dying. Since according to the Christian concept of life death is not the end of life's course, but should rather have a formative influence on the whole life through its resurrecting call, so the entire life in its individuality is consecrated through the consecration of its last moment.

This is the eucharistically centred unity of the seven sacraments. One group forms and renews the Church, so that in the confrontation of the ordained and the lay people is found the confrontation of Christ who offers and the Church who co-offers. The other group takes human existence in its individuality and community and opens it to participation in the sacrifice of Christ which is made present in the eucharistic celebration of the Church.

THE CHURCH AS THE BASIC SACRAMENT

Now from the thoughts developed so far let us turn back again to look at the nature and meaning of the Church itself. What was said about the Church as a sign of our salvation in the first chapter, is now seen in a new light. As the excerpt quoted earlier from *Poetry and Truth* shows, Goethe himself had already sensed the relationship: 'The Christian must be accustomed to see the interior religion of the heart and the external religion of the Church as one complete unity, as a great common sacrament, that can be divided into many different parts each of which gives its own holiness, indestructibility and immortality.'

The Misconception of the Relation between Church and Sacraments

The relationship between the Church and the celebration of the individual sacraments is often mistakenly characterized by the expression of the Church 'having to administer' the sacraments. It is true that the Church has to administer the sacraments: this is undeniable. But this expression is likely to evoke the impression of a warehouse where the utensils and tools are kept in order to be handed out by the 'administrator' to the man who can show his right to use them. It is not the man's interest in the manager of the warehouse which moves him to go there; his interest is exclusively in the objects which he wants to use. The warehouse interests him only because of the objects stored there; and the manager only because he can give or deny access. For the warehouse manager on the other hand, the objects have no meaning, except that the management of them brings him his livelihood.

Is it the same with the 'administering' of the sacraments by the Church? Many of our contemporaries, practicing churchgoers at that, have no difficulties in thinking this way. What is operating here is only a very common misunderstanding as to what religion and the role of the Church in it really is. It is thought necessary to find a contradiction between the personal, individual, interior life of religion and the anonymous, impersonal, institutional, organizational, and external character of the Church. Whoever attributes the nature of religion to the personal decision of a subjective conscience alone, seeing the standing of the individual before the one God as an interior experience which scorns all materiality, can naturally only understand the service of the Church as a support coming from the outside—as a ' guardianship by God ' that will one day make itself superfluous.

But even when one of these religious individualists is willing to concretize his encounter with God in the reception of the sacraments, because he believes in their being instituted by Jesus Christ, he only thinks of God as being hidden in the sacramental wrapping. He puts up with the Church only because there must be a legitimate authority to administer this sacrament instituted by Christ. He is ready to acknowledge the Church and its functionaries as administrators of the sacraments and instructors in the proper reception of the sacraments in an appropriately moral life. But he cannot easily adapt to the fact that all his life should be bound to this administrative and educational activity of the Church. He always feels that somehow the time will come when he does not need such administrative agency for the adult practice of his religion. Thus the Church and its spiritual authority is almost necessarily seen as a bothersome intermediary.

The Church and the Individual Sacraments

In truth, the Church has a very interior and essential relationship with that salvation which man aspires to when he received the sacraments. We have already established that the sacraments include the individual-communal life and they continually vitalize the Church so that in the encounter of the priest representing Christ and the participating lay community, the sacramental celebration of Christ's sacrifice becomes possible. At the same time we determined that the sacramental celebration of Christ's sacrifice is the life centre of the Church, in which its most profound meaning is realized. If this is true, the Church is not merely concerned with the orderly and legitimate administration of the sacraments. It is not merely a supervisor of actions whose meaning is to make God present to the individual person. We must not interpret the role of the Church in administering the sacraments the same as the role of the priest in the marriage ceremony. There he ' witnesses,' as the juridical term puts it, he just stands by. When the believer encounters Christ the Lord in the sacraments, the Church does not just stand by; it does not just administer the sacramental rites so that in the process Christ and the believer find each other in the Church. Rather, the sacramental Church joins itself to man in the individual sacraments and holds him in itself, in the Church as the fundamental sacrament, just as a man carries something in physical closeness within the clasp of his arms. All sacraments have the initial and direct effect of bringing man, for the first time or in a new way, into a living union with the Church itself. First, baptism, through the indelible sign, makes man a member of the mystical body of Christ which is the Church. Confirmation completes this membership and transforms it into the conscious and adult confrontation with the secular world. Holy orders puts the priest in the special place within the Church from which he can bring Christ, the bridegroom, to a visible meeting with his bridal community. The sacrament of penance restores peace with the Church which man lost by sin—an action directed against the nature of the Church. Marriage as an indissoluble bond is an image of the Church bound to Christ in faithfulness. Finally, the sacrament of anointing gives the sick person the important consecration and responsibility, in sickness or—as God wills—in death, to 'proclaim the death of the Lord until he comes,' (1 *Cor.* 11: 26), applying Paul's words about the eucharistic feast which also can be used here.

Since the Holy Spirit, in the power of grace, animates the body of the Church as a soul, therefore man's entering into the Church anew in the sacraments—if he brings to the encounter the proper disposition—is at the same time an immersion into the living union with God, that is, into grace. The new reality in the Church and in grace, both of which are effected by the sacraments, are not, of course, the same. It can even be that one has a place in the Church but does not receive grace. Nevertheless, the two are not to be thought of simply as two parallel effects. Rather, one is contained in the other as the soul is contained in the body. The Church is God's will to save, made visible by the institution of Christ. The individual sacramental acts gather man into the life sphere of the Church. Once brought in, man receives the grace-full life of the community with the triune God, who exists in the Church as its life principle. As the source sacrament, the Church is a sign of the gracious God, as the body is a sign of the soul that animates it. When one is admitted into the body of the Church, he immerses himself in the life of God which permeates the whole body of the Church, as was demonstrated by storm and fire on the day of Pentecost. The condition is: That the reception of the sacraments is accompanied by the interior personal decision of the person receiving them.

Chapter Four

Sacraments and Personal Commitment

Perhaps it is the self-defence of the spirit in the age of the masses, the struggle of freedom against the tyranny of the mass mentality: Modern man watches jealously over the recognition of his personalness. Personalism has become a slogan in the spiritual turmoil of our times. Even though it goes without saying that his avowed concern is often false, the basis for it is justified. But when personalism is mistaken for individualism, liberty for license, self-fulfilment for self-aggrandizement, it is difficult to be receptive to a sacramental conversion to God.

At the end of his book, *Modern Catholicism*, the Protestant theologian Walther von Loewenich writes: ' On Protestantism is laid the responsibility for the existence of a Christianity that recognized the truth of the Gospels and at the same time takes seriously the general scientific concern for truth of the present time.' [1] He sees this scientific concern for the truth endangered in Catholicism. For he has expressly granted in his book that Catholic Christianity lives from the Gospel. The intellectual obligation, however, is something which man today, anxious to preserve the rights of the person, sees endangered by the relationship with Church and the sacraments. The respect of the spirit in face of objective truth, the freedom of will in the affairs of the world, do not seem at home in the sacramental sphere of the Church.

In the last chapter we shall investigate the reasons which this fear seems to find in the sacramental faith of our Church. We start with two points of view. First of all, the effect of the sacrament seems to infringe on the personal dignity of both the holy God and independent man. We shall treat of this in the first part. Secondly, the dignity of the human person, attracted by the privilege of freedom, feels diminished by the bond of man to Church and the sacraments, considered necessary for salvation. This we shall discuss in the second part.

[1] Witten, 1956, p. 417.

SACRAMENTAL 'MAGIC' AND PERSONAL DEVELOPMENT

Personal Responsibility

It need not be only his own person that man is concerned about when he is offered salvation through the sacraments. The preservation of the personal dignity of the holy God also seems to be endangered in sacramental religiosity. This concern might touch on two points.

First we must consider the reproach which has been voiced down through the ages and which even today still characterizes the dialogue between denominations: It is an attempt to influence the infinite God by means of a creature. That man wishes to influence God as a cause at all is considered presumptuous. Man may turn to God as a petitioner. This is not actually a causal influencing of the infinite God but admission of one's own insufficiency and need of assistance. It is therefore an acknowledgement by man of himself as he is here and now; it is the expression of confident hope in the readiness of the merciful God to help; it is, finally, an acknowledgement of faith in God's power to help in this particular situation. In the sacrament, however, man does not seem to hope, but to be sure of the effect of grace; he does not deliver himself to God's mercy, confessing his own inability, but seems to want to extort a gift from God in the magical performance of a human action.

When one considers the natural inadequacy of the means used in this ‘ coercion of God,’ the concern about the sacraments as magic and sorcery increases. What can the pouring of water, the anointing with oil, the feeding with bread and wine mean for the infinite God? The Old Testament psalmist attributes these words to him: ‘ Mine are all the animals of the forests, beasts by the thousand on my mountains. I know all the birds of the air, and whatever stirs in the plains belongs to me. If I were hungry, I should not tell you, for mine are the world and its fullness.’ And furthermore God demands: ‘ Then call upon me in time of distress; I will rescue you, and you shall glorify me ’ (*Psalm* 49: 10–15). The early Church writers were familiar with these ideas. Thus Tertullian writes at the beginning of the third century in his treatise on baptism: ‘ Nothing hardens the heart of man as the simpleness of God’s works, which one sees in the act, and the glory which is promised in the effect.’ But at the same time he sees in this discrepancy a reflection of the simplicity and the power of God: ‘ We too wonder, but because we believe. The disbeliever wonders without believing. His wonderment considers simpleness as emptiness and the glorious as impossible.'

The fears of the personalist seem to be related to the following: All too often are the sacraments described only as instrumental sources of grace. And thereby the danger results of considering that grace which is imparted by the sacrament as separate from God, as a gift detached from him. This grace, as a thing given to man, or administered to him as a kind of medicine to strengthen him, seems now to fall to the lot of man, no longer too much connected with God. Thus the sacramental act of mediating salvation seems to put a thing in place of God. And this contemporary man —to the extent that he is still religious and senses what the grace of God is—cannot accept.

But even more than with God's untouchable person, personalism is concerned with the personal rights of man himself which seem to be endangered by the bond with the sacraments. Here the tendency of the late medieval and early modern theologians to interpret the saving power of sacraments in terms of cause and effect is a danger which must be taken seriously. To be sure, the magisterium of the Church, especially the Council of Trent, prefers to express the salvific meaning of the sacraments in the words, they confer grace (*conferunt*), or contain it (*continent*).[2] It is also said

[2] Denzinger, 849–851.

that baptism is the 'instrumental cause' of the 'grace of justification,'[3] but it is also clearly pointed out that the sacraments impart that kind of grace which is represented by sign and symbol. The very first part of the thesis on the sacraments in the *Summa Theologica* of St Thomas of Aquinas confirms that the sacraments belong in the category of signs.[4] With this the sacrament is clearly interpreted as an appeal to the personal commitment of man. The sacrament is a sign inasmuch as it presents to man's mind a symbolic representation of invisible grace, so that he can decide for or against it. According to ancient tradition the sacrament is at the same time a sign by which man expresses his attitude of faith before God and the Church, the attitude which is hidden deep within him, and which should be made tangible and visible by the reception of the sacraments. In modern sacramental theology the idea of the symbolic character of the sacraments unfortunately has been overshadowed by the exaggerated cause and effect thinking. This means that there is a danger that the man to whom the sacrament is imparted will be regarded only as an object for the salvation activity of the official Church. The essential receptive disposition of the faithful

[3] Ibid. 799; ibid. 718.

[4] *S. Theol.* III, Question 60, art 1.

before the dispenser of the sacrament who represents Christ can be easily mistaken for passivity, something which contemporary man, intent on deed and decision, may resent as unworthy of him.

The Person in the Sacrament

We must take the concerns expressed in these objections seriously and seek to answer them with a true understanding of the mediating action of the sacraments. By answering the following three questions we may be able to shed some light on the subject. First, what actually produced the effect of the sacrament? Second, what is this effect, the grace, which results from the sacrament? And third, what is the personal attitude of man when he receives the sacrament?

First then we ask about the source from which the effect of the sacraments is derived. We must exclude the suspicion of magic and sorcery, which the theological term *ex opere operato* (loosely translated as, ' based on the completion of the sacramental action ') seems to suggest. In theology, as indeed in other sciences, the language of the experts has developed into a sort of professional jargon which hides rather than explains the meaning to the unitiated. We must above all observe two things if we want to understand the expression *ex opere operato* correctly and without magical overtones.

First, the concept *ex opere operato* stands in opposition to another way in which the operation of grace through the sacraments can be presented. *Ex opere operato* means primarily NOT *ex opere operantis*, that is, not depending on the merit of the human performance. One wonders if the reformers of the sixteenth century, as well as Protestant Christians today who so often fear the magic in the Catholic teaching on the sacraments, have realized actually how much their own basic demands are fulfilled here. The stress on the sacraments imparting grace *ex opere operato* prevents the misconception, such as that found in the Pelagian heresy in the early days of the Church, that man could obtain grace through the merits of his own works, that is, *ex opere operantis*. In opposition to this, the sacrament stresses that grace is not obtained as a result of human action on God, but through the operation of a sign of God's promise instituted by him.

Furthermore, we must investigate the meaning of the word *opus*, work, from which the concept *ex opere operato* derives grace. Does it really mean that the minimal sacral action which the imparter of the sacrament gives and the receiver accepts actually imparts divine life? This kind of superstitution which holds that the action of a creature could have a determining effect on God has already been refuted by the early Church Fathers. Because God is effectively present in the sacramental act, it has the power to impart God. 'So believe therefore,' St Ambrose writes,[5] 'that God is present there. You believe in his effect, but you do not believe in his presence. But how could he be effective if he were not present?' There is also the often repeated assurance that the effect of baptism is independent of the merit of the person who administers it, because it is Christ who baptizes. 'The priest,' St John Chrysostom assures us, 'lends his tongue and offers his hand to serve.'[6] Thus the great theologian of the nineteenth century, Johann Adam Möhler could rightly add (though not quite correctly from the history of the terminology) *a Christo*, to the *ex opere operato.*[7] From the power of the work *of Christ*, which is represented and contained in them, the sacraments impart the grace of God.

What became clear in the central sacraments of baptism and eucharist in the New Testament, an analogy of faith also ascribes to the other sacraments. They present, under different aspects, the sacrifice which Christ performed; these are

[5] De mysteriis, Cao. 3, No. 8, ML 16, 391.
[6] St John's Gospel 86, 4. MG 59, 472.
[7] *Symbolik*, 1. Buch, 4. Kap. p. 28.

hidden under symbolic covering but at the same time are discernible in our visible present for those instructed in the faith. When using the expression *ex opere operato* we are referring to the sacramental act which is accomplished here: we mean the redemptive work of Christ contained in it like a soul in a body. In receiving the sacrament we confidently call upon the sacrifice of Christ as the source of all grace which we hold in our hand, so to speak, in the external form of the sacrament. It is not only in a juridical sense that the receiver of the sacraments calls on Christ's sacrifice; and not only by reminding God of a fact which lies buried in the historical past. Rather he holds the sacrifice of Christ in sacramental form in his hand now as his own sacrifice too, and he shows it to God, his Father.

It is then infallibly certain that God will not deny to man who comes to him in the sacrifice of Christ that return gift of himself which we call grace. This is not because God is obligated to us men, but rather to his Son whom he caused to become man in fulfilment of a promise and whose sacrifice he has accepted as a pledge for us all.

The second question was: What is the nature of this grace which we owe to the sacraments? Is it really something as material as one fears? Here again we must learn to proceed with caution when we present the sacraments as instruments for the production of grace. It never can be a question of man being treated as mere matter. The sacramental imparting of grace does not abolish the interpersonal relation between God and man, nor the personal encounter of the two, but acts as mediator.

If we accept what we said above, the whole argument loses much of its difficulty. What happens when man, in the reception of the sacraments, calls upon the sacrifice of Christ before God and even enters into this sacrifice? What actually happens is a gift of man to God through invoking the sacrificial immolation of Christ.

Grace is God's answer to the offering of his Son—in which indeed the offering of man is included. It is so much the answer to it, that grace has the same nature, if also in an infinitely more complete way: Grace is God's gift of himself to man, as the sacrifice was man's gift of self to God in the God-man. In grace God himself in a certain sense enters man as a life principle, to sanctify him from the inside out in a way which the Church Fathers called divinization.

Finally, the third question follows: How should man behave personally in the sacrament? The question can be concretely formulated in this way:

Does not the operation of the sacrament *ex opere operato*, insofar as it stands in opposition to man's own initiative, have the effect of repressing the decision of the person in a way that would make belief in the sacrament difficult for one who jealously watches over the maturity of his personality?

Here we must consider that in the conceptual differentiation between *ex opere operato* and *ex opere operantis* the accent is really on the '*ex*.' In other words, we are not by any means saying that the *opus operantis*—that which man brings to the sacrament from his own personal commitment—is unimportant and may remain unnoticed. We only say that the human performance is not the origin or source, *ex qua*, from which grace originates. Indeed, the action of the sacrifice of Christ to the eternal God that is hidden in the sacrament will not be fruitful in man unless his reception of the sacrament is also a symbol and expression of his actually existing *opus operantis*, his personally offered gift to God. The Council of Trent has stated that grace is given to man 'according to the amount the Holy Spirit imparts to the individual, as he wills, and according to man's own readiness and cooperation.'[8] This is a clear and unquestionable appeal to the human person and

[8] Denzinger, 799.

his decision. This appeal to man's decision has its visible forcefulness in the performance of the sacraments. For the sacraments are the sources of grace.

But this also follows from the nature and meaning of the sacraments themselves. They effect their mediation of grace as signs. They are objective instruments and at the same time representational means of expression. Thus we must not overlook the intent which is inherent in each sign and symbol. Signs only exist where there are persons to be addressed who can interpret them and in whom the effect represented by the signs can operate. The imparting of the sacrament which contains grace, makes a silent appeal to man's decision. Reception of this sacrament should be not only symbol and expression of the fact that God communicates in grace with man, but that man gives himself to God. The sacrament, therefore, is an expression for the turning-to-each-other of two who might also close themselves off from each other. What can be more personal than this communication between God and man?

SACRAMENTAL BOND AND PERSONAL FREEDOM

There is something else that freedom-conscious man is perhaps even more sensitive to than the things we have discussed so far. Even the person who is receptive to religion does not easily understand that this turning to God should be tied to an organized institution. In order to do justice to this question, we shall examine it in three steps.

The Church and the Individual

The age of mass civilization and disciplined organization easily leads to the temptation, even in the sphere of the Church, to put organization above spirit, legality above love, mass conformity above the decision of the individual. Combatting this, however, leads to the opposite temptation: To make the religious sphere—which is perhaps the only area remaining that can be experienced privately—completely private, and that means in this case to individualize it, and to cultivate the life before God with all possible interiority, ignoring the material aspects. How difficult it will be then to understand that in the religious sphere too John Donne's words apply: ' No man is an island, entire of itself. Every man is a piece of the continent, a part of the domain.'[9] One easily forgets that the life before God must remain human, that is, corporal. In the Church the whole man encounters God. Therefore all the elements which determine human existence must be raised up in the redeeming infusion by the Holy Spirit in the Church. Spirit and body, individuality and community, God-centredness and world involvement: into all this the incarnate son of God extends himself from his own individual God-man personality into the whole Church, so that even in this respect the Church is a *pleroma*, the fullness of Christ. Thus the whole New Testament is shot through with indications that Christ must actualize his turning to God by his turning to men. The community relationship must remain an enduring element in the life before God as it is in the natural existence of man.

Community and Society in the Church

But this does not make the founding of a Church necessary, and so we proceed to the second phase of our inquiry. If man must bring his community sense to the Christian encounter with God, why can it not be the way many Utopian theologians, such as the followers of Rudolf Sohm,[10] wish—

[9] John Donne (1572–1631).
[10] *Wesen und Ursprung des Katholizismus*, Leipzig, 1909.

the way they maintain is in reality the meaning of the New Testament *ecclesia*: [11] Is it not possible that the redeemed community might be formed from the many individual followers who respond to the call of Christ in the Holy Spirit? Is it not possible that the Church could be assembled from the spontaneous decision of individuals, spurred on by grace, and become a Church as a pure community of persons which needs no organization because it lives in the Holy Spirit? Why must the community of the followers of Christ be realized through the organization of the Church? Why must the fact that the community aspect of human existence is also redeemed result in an institution of persons deciding individually? Why does the Church have to be instituted instead of resulting from the will of many individuals? Even more: Why can the community aspect of redeemed mankind take form only in a universal society, which is therefore called the Catholic Church? The human person would like to exercise his creative freedom in deciding anew to form the community of faithful around Christ, instead of giving his ' yes ' to a community already formed.

Now let us consider once more what we have established about the Church as a sacramental sign. It is not only a sheltering enclosure which protects

[11] Emil Brunner, *The Misunderstanding of the Church*, Westminster, 1953.

the personal decision of the individuals against outside attack. This enveloping function is also exercised in helping man, transfixed by God's grace, to discover his own form of expression for going to God. The Church is the organism vitalized by the spirit of God in whose life functions men can give expression to their encounter with the infinite God in such a way that they find certain acceptance.

It may perhaps be asked: Is it not part of the freedom and spontaneity of the human individual to choose his own fitting symbols of expression in the encounter with another person? In the encounter of man to man, it is true that one first takes an interior attitude towards the other, and that this inner attitude then seeks a fitting form of expression which expresses itself and nothing else. But even in interpersonal relations this freedom of the form of expression is very restricted. Certainly the same words sound different, according to the mouth and heart from which they come. But this difference is only a variation of an essentially predetermined form of expression which is given a personal mark by the meaning put into it by the individual. The handshake with which two people greet each other does differ from person to person. But it remains only a handshake.

In this predetermination of the basic form of expression it is obvious that the individuals who encounter each other recognize and actualize a pre-existing community of mankind.

This, then, is the meaning of the bond of religious community relationship to the Church as a society: The God-encounter of the community-minded man is predetermined by the institution of the God-man into a certain social form. And in the encounter with God, man has the choice of saying ' yes ' to the form of expression proposed by Christ, in a more or less personal way, because he should acknowledge the sovereignity and initiative of the divine partner.

The fact that one can find the expression of the encounter with God only in an area removed from the world and the commonplace demonstrates God's transcendence and other-worldliness and the supernatural, grace-full character of the living community with him.

Salvation Outside the Church

If all this is affirmed in faith, the champion of the human person still has as a third step the thorny question concerning the fate of those who in their personal attitude are receptive to God, but through no fault of their own have not found the way into the visible Church. We are inclined to ask: Is their personal decision of so little account that it remains fruitless because of the lack of official membership in the Church? This is what the ancient principle '*extra ecclesiam nulla salus*' seems to say. We must admit that the interpretation of this principle still has its difficulties in our day. This much, however, may be considered settled: The official Church does not categorically maintain that all men, unless they are within the visible and sheltering Church, must drown in the deluge of sin. When an American Jesuit a few years ago defended this narrow interpretation of the principle of '*extra ecclesiam nulla salus*,' the highest magisterium in the Church, the Holy Office in Rome, suspended the priest and excommunicated him.[12] And thus a significant paradox emerged: excessive advocacy of the need for belonging to the Church in order to be saved resulted, in this case, in the loss of membership in that Church.

The right interpretation of the truth of faith that salvation may be gained only through the Church and its sacramental life is perhaps made more difficult by a too physical understanding of the concept of 'necessity.' Theological terminology calls the need for belonging to the Church

[12] Cf. A. Hoffman, O.P., 'Die Heilsnotwendigkeit der Kirche nach einer authentischen Erkla' rung des Hl. Offiziums *Die neue Ordnung*. (1953).

in the plan of salvation, a *necessitas medii* (a necessity of means). It is therefore not simply a *necessitas praecepti*, that is, a necessity given through positive command, not already in a physical relationship to an objective order. What does it mean then when the Church and its sacramental life is called a necessary 'means' for obtaining salvation? Is this really to be understood in the sense of physical effect, as the use of an instrument is necessary to produce a certain result? We have already seen that grace can be only very inadequately interpreted as a physical effect which God produces in the human 'material' by means of the sacrament; it is much better understood as the personal self-communication of God into the heart of the human person. The Church and the sacraments might also be better understood as the necessary 'means' of salvation in the sense of the 'means of expression,' which would then put the whole matter on a more personal level.

Let us try to illustrate this with an example from everyday life. In order for two people to associate with each other, they must know how to speak. And if their native language is different they must seek a common language to make themselves understood. The community of a language in which one can express himself and the other can understand him is a necessity for the exchange between them. It is the indispensable 'means of expression.' And yet no one will refuse to respect the halting attempts of a child to express himself in conversation. The foreigner's stumbling way of speaking might be conspicuous, but one will not refuse to answer him for this reason. Yet it remains true that the ability to speak is a necessary means of exchange. No one can say that inner goodwill is sufficient for an exchange, with no need for a means of communication. A basic, rudimentary store of understandable expressions is necessary.

We have seen that the Church is instituted by the Lord as a sacred place and sign whose life functions are the only legitimate means of expression for the mutual offering of God and man. In the institution of Christ God has exercised his absolute right over his partner to determine the language in which the communication takes place. As evidence of the fact that God's will to save has made it possible for man to speak to God through Christ, he has determined the sign by which this conversation of salvation must be conducted. This does not preclude the fact that there remains beyond the limits set by God's institution a wider area for the free and individual formation of human conversation with God.

Now, there are many people who in their

personal attitude and conduct are truly receptive to communication with God. But, through no fault of their own, they have not found the one valid area for this exchange and the only legitimate means of expression, the sacramental life of the Church. Yet they are not completely without means of expression, not without the rudimentary elements for valid means of communication. They have baptism, and a certain claim to real 'churchness.' Or, if they are not baptized, they still possess human nature which makes them to a certain extent akin to the God-man. They are not in the ark, out of the flood, but they sit on the edge or hang from the side. Through these common rudiments of faith, their personal attitude before God and salvation is not without some means of communication which in its fullness is found only in the Church. Would God not take this stammering conversation with him for full communication if man has not attained it, through no fault of his own? We hope so, at least, and the Church itself encourages us to do so.

The nature and meaning of the Church and the sacraments demand from us an attitude that is equally removed from the false, either-or kind of perfectionism that can only discourage us in facing the world, and the false indifferentism and relativism which puts the Church and sacraments as objects of free human choice alongside other denominations and religions, even agnosticism. We must not believe, on the one hand, that all is lost or that the Church is not bringing salvation to all the world as long as the masses are not visibly obedient children. On the other hand, we must not regard the encounter with God through a rudimentary incorporation into the Church as sufficient and equal to the full actualization of the Church instituted by Christ. The stammering of the child seeks for the perfect language, and hanging on to the rim of the ark indicates the need to be in it. One who knows the way to the Church and the sacramental life and deliberately refuses it continues to stammer without really being a child any more. One who prefers hanging on to the rim of the ark to being received into the Church will live a compromise which is impossible to sustain for long.

We must never tire of gathering men into the whole and full Church with its life in word and sacrament, and we must above all see to it that our life itself represents the Church as a true sign of salvation.

M. H. GILL AND SON LTD., PRINTERS, DUBLIN